READING PEOPLE:

A MASTER HYPNO-THERAPIST'S GUIDE TO UNDERSTANDING PEOPLE IN 60 SECONDS!

Sanjay Burman M.HT

BURMANBOOKS

Published by BurmanBooks Inc.
260 Queens Quay West
Suite 904
Toronto, Ontario
Canada M5J 2N3

Cover and interior design:
Jack Steiner Graphic Design

Editing:
Jean Keating

Distribution:
Trumedia Group
c/o Ingram Publisher Services
14 Ingram Blvd.
LaVergne, TN 37086

ISBN 978-1-897404-18-8

Printed and bound in Canada

To All the teachers and mentors in my life.
I have realized only recently that most go through life
without a single mentor, and yet,
I have too many to mention.
Thank you.

Acknowledgements

My support team Bruce Rosenberg (best friend and lawyer), John Manakaros (Project Manager and Sanjay's Rabbi), Jack Steiner, Marc Doucet, David Wilk, Alex Barbieri and Joe Carlos.

I would also like to thank Tommy Hilfiger, Annie Lamarre, Lauren Cracower, Dr. William Prusin as strong supporters. Howard Schultz (not the Starbucks dude) for making me realize a few years ago just how important body language was. Phil Kent, David Kent who really are my older brothers, Rick Nicita and Ari Emanuel for patience and teaching me. Harvey Simon and Don Mottin for their hypnosis training. Jacquie Jordan for her kindness. Mr. And Mrs. Scott for the yummy recipe at the end!

To my parents, thank you for having sex. Had you not, someone else would take credit for this book.

And to my dear editor, Jean Keating. I like to give credit where credit is due. She worked hard on making me look intelligent. Thank you.

And thank you to those who gave me the material for this book just by being themselves. Ronnie,

Barbara, Tim, Harriet, Chantelle, Deanna, Joy, Chinh, Chadd, Marigold, John, Antonietta, Desiree, Christine, Chris, Tanya S., Tanya M., Timothy, Bruce, John, Scott, Wendy, Giselle, Ryan and my parents.

Contents

Introduction: Three Rules / ix

SECTION ONE: Observe and Assess

CHAPTER 1: My Chaos Theory / 2

CHAPTER 2: Sizing someone up / 8

CHAPTER 3: See and hear / 34

CHAPTER 4: You know it's a lie when… / 49

CHAPTER 5: You know they are into you when… / 55

CHAPTER 6: You know where you stand in negotiations when… / 59

CHAPTER 7: Assault victims and the after effects / 65

CHAPTER 8: Self Sabotage / 83

SECTION TWO: Get What You Want

Introduction: Reaching Your Goal/ 93

CHAPTER 1: Mirroring to establish rapport / 96

CHAPTER 2: The Preacher is NOT the Teacher / 108

CHAPTER 3: The Addiction Factor / 106

CHAPTER 4: Balance / 109

CHAPTER 5: Success? No way! / 111

CHAPTER 6: The word "No" is magical / 114

CHAPTER 7: Our Unknown Heaven / 117

JOURNAL EXERCISE / 123

Introduction

Reading people has two equally significant requirements. The first is seeing others, while the second is truly seeing yourself. A reason to use these techniques would be to avoid mistakes that can be averted.

For instance, there was a girl I was crazy about. On her birthday, I set up an entire day of fun. I had her meet me in the morning and took her north of the city to the sugar- bush to sample fresh maple syrup. Then we went to a spa where she got a massage, and back to my place where I had prepared dinner. Because she had recently graduated from university, I bought her a watch and to throw her off put it in a cigar box. When I gave her the box, she burst out into tears... not the tears of joy, but sadness! She looked at me and said that the last person she had smoked a cigar with, was her ex-boyfriend and realizes she still has feelings for him! This was like stepping in cow shit and no water hose in sight. In fact, getting her to even open the box proved to be a task. When I did, I might as well have thrown the watch out the window since all the attention was still on the cigar box. I didn't have the heart to tell her I had the watch engraved telling her I loved her.

After not having access to a time machine, I was able to turn the situation around by being able to read her reactions and know the words that would most empower her to move out of that emotional state. By the end, she was cradled in my lap and her snot on my shirt. It just doesn't get better than that!

And yes, I'm more romantic than the cover would lead you to believe.

This book will give you the tools to accomplish both feats. If, and only if, you can follow these three rules.

1. Eliminate your ego.
2. Be observant. You have two ears and one mouth for a reason. Shut up and listen.
3. The biggest mistake you can make is thinking you know yourself. You don't.

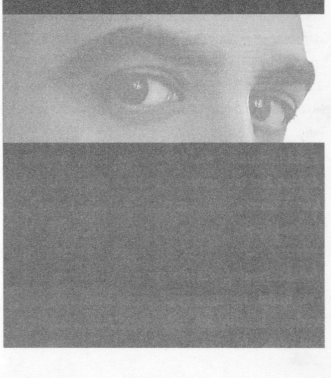

SECTION ONE

Observe
& Assess

CHAPTER ONE

My Chaos Theory

The first step to reading people is to understand why they do the things that you hate. Upon understanding this, they will no longer upset you, since you will understand the motivation behind their actions. Either that, or you will know how to attack their insecurities until they crawl into a fetal position and weep to the sounds of Kumbaya. Just kidding...well, not really.

'What you repress, another will express', Dr. John Demartini said so eloquently. So, for every emotion that you hold back, someone else is prepared to express it. Any habit, emotion or action that is brought about by someone that irritates you is a repressed mirror inside of you. Change what *you* repress and watch how the dynamic between you and the person changes. The action, emotion or habit will either dissipate, or that person will stop coming around you as often. Most importantly, what aggravated you before will no longer aggravate you now.

I was with a banker who was in charge of an investment division. His clothing was pristine, hair perfectly set, and a tan that looked natural. After analyzing him, I discovered he was insecure in his job and his image was his mask. Either that, or Fabio was his idol. Sure enough, his daughter had assumed his suppressed qualities by not achieving her potential and being afraid of her image. He said that she was a good athlete but that she was not achieving her full potential, almost like she was afraid of what other people think. Rather than address his own issues, he focused on hers.

Also consider the incredibly clean person married to the incredibly dirty person, or the overachiever married to the underachiever. You wonder how that happened! I see my ex with her present husband and I have to read this book aloud just to make sense of it! It is not as simple as opposites attract. Each partner is suppressing the opposing aspect of the other person's personality. The only way they can express it is by getting involved with somebody that contains it. It's a form of punishing the other person for your own sins. Sounds deep and religious almost! But human dynamics are just that simple.

The question is how do we change that? Are we stuck with a mate who is unorganized and filthy? The answer is no. The way to change that quality in the person is to change the quality you don't like in them, in yourself.

If you've been cheated on or abused, think about how you may have done the same to someone else. Let's take a woman who always gets into abusive relationships. The first question is: who did she abuse to get into the vicious cycle? As harsh as it sounds, the law stays the same. Could it be that she has been accepting of those relationships because she has been abusing herself? Or, could it be that she expresses herself in an abusive manner to her best friend?

The thing about the chaos theory is, it can also work for you. The famous saying, "You have to spend money to make money", doesn't only work in an economical sense, but also, in a natural sense according to the laws of the universe. The basic law of physics is whatever goes up must come down, every action has a like reaction.

I had a problem with an assistant to someone I was working with. You should always be very good to those who work as assistants to executives. They can get you in the door. This assistant was giving me a hard time and preventing me from reaching my goals. My lawyer and I were having lunch and he said 'Just go to the executive and tell him what is going on behind his back!' I thought about the chaos theory and I realized it would only cause problems. So, instead, on my trip to India, I bought her a silk scarf. It didn't cost much there, but the return on the investment was 400%. She became my best friend and biggest ally. She was fired 3 weeks later. Maybe the moral of the lesson is to smother the person with kindness no matter how harsh they have been, and they will either quit or get fired? Not quite, but they will quit getting in your way.

There are no victims in the game of reading people, there are only players, and there are no loopholes. The chaos theory applies to everything and everyone. This is why learning the rules is so important. No gesture, look, word or action is done by mistake. Maybe not consciously, but the brain's sub-conscious is 10 times more powerful than our conscious brain.

As I was writing this book, someone I had just ended a relationship with 3 weeks ago called my cell phone. As I went to answer it and saw her name (you know who you are), she had just hung up. Well, I laughed because she may say she did it by mistake and she may be right...consciously. Subconsciously she might have thought about me for some time, or had an experience that reminded her of something I said and her finger 'accidentally' called.

I was teaching a hypnosis class and showing people in the class how easy it is to read them by doing it in less than 60 seconds, when one of the students asked if I might be reading too much into it. I turned to her and replied that she is someone who probably suppresses bad events or thoughts and tries to deflect conflict by hoping it will fix itself. She was taken aback but ultimately, she confirmed my claim.

The Universe's law is always black or white. By trying to facilitate a grey, you're only cheating and victimizing yourself, while losing the opportunity to gain. A grey attempt would only be your ego trying to achieve a fictional superior stance that doesn't exist. You achieve an authentic superior stance when you can read and understand others, and identify strengths and weaknesses in yourself. The is precisely what this book aims to teach you.

CHAPTER TWO

Sizing someone up

Pictures never lie. It sees what it sees, good or bad.

The people that never show their teeth when smiling are fascinating because they usually love being in pictures, but are always hiding something. Sometimes its braces or unhealthy teeth, or sometimes it's as significant as their motives.

Then there are those who don't even really smile. They use their facial muscles to move the sides of their lips up, but it's not a smile. A real smile has wrinkles or 'crow's feet' on the outer sides of the eyes, while the creases around the mouth show. Look at press pictures of me. I hate them so much and make an effort to smile. But if you look at my eyes, you will not see wrinkles on the sides of them, instead, you will see an uncomfortable glance from my eyes. Another great example would be stars walking the red carpet. Most of them would rather eat my mother's brussel sprouts than be photographed in an uncomfortable surrounding like caged animals. (If you didn't get it, my mother's brussel sprouts are not good.)

People who are not genuinely happy, smile the same way in every picture. In fact if you put all their pictures together, and flip through them quickly, the background and people around them change, but their face never does! It's quite interesting actually. Their face represents their lives to themselves, boring and uninspiring. Most of my high school pictures are like that. Go through Facebook pictures and you will see great examples.

Profile pictures are particularly insightful. Some of us profile only our face, which could mean that we aren't happy with the state of our bodies, and some profile our best features. Some guys flex their abs but do not show their faces, or some women will show major cleavage, and only part of their face. This is obviously to make up for what they feel is their lacking qualities.

However, keep in mind the chaos theory. Behind what is clearly expressed often lies an incongruent truth. A great example is Pamela Anderson. If you look at early pictures of her in Vancouver, she was a tomboy. As she got into

Playboy and started to crave the spotlight and attention, she got bigger breast implants, her hair got bigger and bigger (I guess to balance), and she became bimboish, even though she is a marketing genius. Now, in interviews she can't stop playing with her hair. She puts it over her shoulder, tosses it back, then over and then back. Most would call her vain, when really, she is just insecure.

People that fixate on their bodies are not only insecure, they are often extremists. I dated a girl who was a personal trainer, and she made me nuts about working out. She had to have only healthy foods, and a healthy lifestyle, including yoga. The repressed side of her was depressed. When she would cry for an hour, instead of dealing with the issue that was causing her pain, she would go for a run.

Most people that are extraordinarily fit are making up for perceived inferiorities. I was coaching a female body builder because she was not achieving her best results and her body was almost giving up. We realized that her bodybuilding was a way of mentally defending herself from her ex-husband who had been physically abusive. She was training so hard and taking steroids not for a mere competition, but rather for self-preservation.

I had another client who was obese. She was very good at her job, very successful, and very well paid. She came to me to deal with emotional issues in her personal life. When she regressed through hypnosis, I found out that she had been raped by an uncle and a boyfriend. The weight gain was an attempt to protect herself by rendering herself unattractive to men. When we addressed the real issue, she lost 60 pounds in two months without even dieting.

Or, look at me. If you look at my pictures, most of them are at functions next to beautiful women. The probable conclusion would be that I was not great with the ladies when I was younger, lacked self confidence and now I am trying to make up for it by showing off how many pretty ladies I know. In actual fact, many women approach me because of what I have worked to become and that makes me incredibly insecure and careful around them. I'm always looking for their ulterior motives. Therefore, if trying to sell to me, using beautiful women would be the wrong angle. If you were going to sell me, the best way to go about it would be a) to show how I can excel (I'm in the self help world, so there must be something in me I'm searching for answers about) or b) offer something reliable (the idea of being able to count on someone or something gives peace to a person trying to achieve).

Don't be too hasty to draw conclusions solely on pictures. Pictures never lie, however, nor do they offer the whole truth. Even if the person doesn't have an obvious issue they are covering up, it's there so spend time talking to them and you will get the truth.

So before attempting to read someone, meet them in person and keep in mind the following:

1. When someone is late and keeps you waiting, it is power play.

They are exercising power over you and showing you how little they think of you. When they come to greet you, never show you have been waiting. Be busy reading, writing or talking on the phone. Make them wait about 30 seconds until you are done your task. If they are more than twenty minutes late, when they arrive, state very politely that you are late for your next meeting and that you will call them to reschedule. Don't call. They will call you. Don't be upset or resentful, since they will read that and dismiss you. Also, if they try to set up another appointment, tell them you will get back to them on that and go home to check your schedule. Show that you are at least reciprocating.

The same thing with telemarketers. Watch those who pick up the phone and say 'hello' three times before the telemarketer starts in. The telemarketer can assess based on your patience, if they have a shot at a sale or completion of a survey. If I say 'hello' and I don't hear a response after a second, I hang up. My mother will continue to say 'hello' for the next 45 minutes.

2. A person's accessories often reveal their insecurities.

How much makeup is a woman wearing? The more she wears, the more insecure she is about her looks. Compliment her on something that is God given. For instance, her eyes or her hair.

Cigars are big, bold and expensive. Thus, cigar smokers want to be recognized. They are often insecure about their past and have faced poverty. Compliment them on their talent, experience or their wisdom.

The bigger the briefcase, the more detailed the individual. The smaller the briefcase, the more direct the individual. The former never forgets. The lattrer is more likely to be temperamental.

If they peer over their glasses to talk to you, they are trying to intimidate you. A person that takes their glasses off to listen or while the room is silent, is thinking. The one who wears sunglasses indoors is insecure and has something to hide. Look at poker players. This doesn't apply to those who just had surgery on their eyes.

It's interesting when you watch someone answer questions that are making them uncomfortable. For instance, I was out for lunch with a high school friend of mine. He was insisting I go to his young son's birthday party which was go-karting and a barbeque. I agreed and then asked if the boy's mother was also invited. The body language that occurred was very interesting because it displayed an uncomfortable reaction to my simple question.

My friend took the drink menu that remains on the table, and started to play with it subtly. He looked down at it when he answered, and looked up at me only after he finished the thought, but not the answer. 'Naw, she doesn't need to be there, she can have her own party for him'. Then he looked up,

'I invited her for the first one after we broke up, but now it's been 6 years'.

The great part was at that moment, the waitress interrupted us. She usually serves us and she thinks the fact that I order a grilled cheese sandwich at a 'corned beef deli' is hilarious. Every time she comes out to talk to us, when I ask her a question, she will look at me and answer...while covering her wedding ring! Every time this happens. Now, I'm not a GQ Model, as you can see from the cover, but my life changed when I removed the hump from my back and came down from the clock tower!

Let's analyze the reactions. My friend who played with the menu and looked down is actually saying that the animosity between him and his ex-wife hasn't been resolved, but there is shame there because he feels sharing a child and having an amicable relationship would probably be easier on the kids, and himself. His ego prevents him from going any further.

The waitress on the other hand, flirts subconsciously and likes the 'feeling of being single'. She isn't going to cheat...just yet anyway. Her marriage has probably hit a dry spell, but not necessarily because of them, just life. Intrigued, I asked her what her husband does. Turns out he is a music engineer teacher, but used to be a waiter up the street. My follow-up question was to ask how often she worked. Her response was 6 days a week. So that being what it is, how much fun do they get to have together? What are they going to do when she has been running around on her feet all day? The relationship is going to take a hit.

3. Pets tell all.

I have a friend who is 33, single, and working two jobs to make just barely enough to live. She is overweight and does whatever she can to avoid relationships. She doesn't like herself or her life. She may deny it but her actions prove otherwise. The cream on the top of this treat is that she has a huge Rottweiler that takes a lot of money to feed. The dog is very smart. The dog knows if she growls or whines, my friend will give her attention.

When my friend and I were watching a movie on the couch, she asked me to move so the dog could sit on her. No kidding! The dog was chewing on a bone while sitting on her. I was busy watching them, so I can't even tell you what movie we were watching. The dog dropped the bone, and my friend picked it up! The dog dropped it again, and she picked it up again. This went on 28 times (yes, I counted). That's when I realized, she is the pet; the dog is the master.

This occurs when you shut down your ability to connect to another human being for fear of being hurt. You transfer that emotion to an animal which won't leave you. There is a man who lives in my building and every time I see him on the elevator, I dread it. His dog could pretty much take a shit on my shoe and he will say in the most effeminate voice 'Poochy, come here. Please? Come on Poochy buddy.' Even the dog looks at him wondering when he will realize that it will never work! We all know people like this. They have lost the desire to connect with human beings and have made the animal human.

A pet's death is devastating to these personality types. I had another friend who kept her dog's dead body lying in the kitchen all day. The body had actually started to get rigor mortis when I got there. She wanted to keep it another night and stuff it. I had to use hypnosis on her subtly for her to hear any reason. She finally had someone collect the dog's body and she and I went out to dinner to get her out of the environment. I also thought that I might run into a well and someone say 'It puts the lotion on the skin', like I'm in *Silence of the Lambs*!

These types of personalities are very loyal and fall very hard in love. They will treat you well, but because of their past history in relationships, you don't want to use or intentionally hurt them, because they will use all their past pain towards going after you. They are also very needy and will want you around a lot, something they get from animals.

Another great way to measure the household is to obsserve the dog. If it is very angry or hyper or even disrespectful to the owner, there is chaos in the household. If the dog is submissive and almost sad, there is an abusive environment in the house, emotional or physical. An ideal household would be where the dog is happy, playful, respectful and gentle.

4. Assess the environment.

When entering a room, whether it is an office or home, look around. A lawyer I knew used to preach about how money was not important to him. On his walls were medieval swords and

Japanese warrior furnishings. This showed me that he was not being honest. Sure enough, my bill with him was outstanding for $322.00. In one week, I had two e-mails and one phone call from him requesting the money. Don't be fooled by what people say.

We decorate our personal environments with how we want to be seen. This is great because we can see a bit about what they want from life. An example would be walking into a house that is filled with Buddha statues, pictures of Shiva or Krishna and self help books displayed on the bookshelf, seeks enlightenment and peace from a chaotic history. This person will most likely bore the shit out of you by preaching Laws of Attraction and so on, but will only practice it themselves when convenient. Most likely they crash the minute something goes wrong, and get depressed.

Let's take for example, a house displaying books about history, politics, philosophy and poetry. This is a person that really wants to be respected and thought of as intelligent. They know a lot, but feel the need to display it thereby showing their biggest insecurity. The best part is books or bookstore gift certificates are the easiest and best gifts to buy them!

In a work environment, you can see how clean or messy their desks are. If the desk is messy, the person is scattered and doesn't remember specifics. If the desk is clean, they only remember the broad strokes and will have to review to see details. Most lawyers or doctors have clean desks and remember the amount you owe them without checking, but have to check files when you ask, 'Why so high?'

5. The Adrenaline Junkie.

We have all seen the adrenaline junkies and some of us wished we could be them. I am reminded of the 'mimbo' (man bimbo)Tony from an episode of Seinfeld. Elaine dates this good looking adventurer that George gets a man-crush on. Tony convinces George to go rock climbing and other ridiculous things, which George does to look cool in Tony's eyes. I have been there.

I came to study adrenaline junkies when I dated one briefly very recently. She skydived, bungee jumped, and all sorts of other crazy things. These types of personalities were also the ones to try drugs, party all night and go to school all day. They drive fast, live fast and in some cases, die fast. Why?

Simple. They are not happy with their lives and

6 out of the 10 I interviewed, had little to no contact with their families. They are depressed to the point that they have to do drastic things in order to feel euphoria. The very interesting thing that I found was, even though they never admitted it outright, many of them had a death wish. I concluded this when 8 out of 10 had attempted or prepared to attempt suicide at a younger age! The idea of the rope possibly breaking, the shoot not opening, or falling 200 feet, was part of the thrill since the worst case scenario (death), wasn't threatening. I noticed with the girl I was dating, when I shared with her the small joys that were constant, and started to get her to smile and laugh more often, her endorphins would kick in, giving her enough 'happy feelings' that she cut out the life threatening adventures.

So when you see an adrenaline junkie, they are physical preachers rather than verbal ones. They will go on and on about how happy they are, how much they love life and yet they prove this by tempting fate, thereby possibly shortening their lives.

This does not apply to those who like the occasional rollercoaster ride, or will try skydiving with an experienced professional. The above description is for those that are constantly pushing the limits.

6. Lisps.

I have found those with lisps suffer from bouts of immaturity. They will initially come off as confident, put together, and focused, but after a very short while of knowing them, their 12 year old subconscious seems to come to life. Such as still living a 'frat' lifestyle, or being in junior high level relationships. The lisp seems to be a method of freezing a lost moment in time. Some of my friends have lisps, and at work they are exceptional, while their personal lives are warm. While that seems commending, a part of their life always seems to be at an early teen stage.

7. Crackberry

The addiction to cell phones, Blackberries and other communication devices doesn't stop for these people. They use their devices during movies, social outings with other people and unfortunately, even while driving.

We laugh and make comments, but it's a true addiction. The addiction isn't with the device itself, it's with the escapism from whatever they are doing. I have interviewed 6 heavy Blackberry addicts, and in all 6 cases, they suffered from bouts of depression. One is very successful at work, pulling in a very large salary, but has no social life and escapes by watching Youtube at a dinner with friends. During two interviews I conducted, both admitted to not having any friends, so they were constantly typing back and forth to 'acquaintances'.

I concluded that this type of personality feels what is happening on the other side of the Blackberry is more important that what is going on in front of them. Messaging also creates a feeling of importance that they normally don't feel, and they can't risk losing it by not instantly replying. Spending time with a Blackberry addict is very difficult since their attention span lasts for only a few seconds. However, to combat your companion's addiction, calmly get up to leave without saying a word. This will provoke their fear that they are insignificant and they will respond immediately. They will put the device away, but only until the addiction kicks in and they succumb to answering all the important people's important questions.

Pay attention to the people that have Blackberries but almost never check it when they are with you. They are much calmer, much more put together, and much more secure with themselves. They also have more depth to their personalities and enjoy life much more.

8. Angry People

Anger comes in all forms.

Uninhibited anger is displayed, of course, when a person snaps and starts yelling or swearing. The easiest way of dealing with this is to bring their energy down to your level, rather than you going up to theirs. Calmly ask: 'Why are you so upset?' The question will prompt a conversation that will divert their minds from what they think they are angry about. From there, push a little more with, "What are you really angry about? If you tell me, maybe I can help you get what you want". They will instantly calm down because anger often spawns from simply not being heard. The alternative, yelling something like, "I can't do anything", will only fuel their anger.

The second and scarier version of anger is inhibited; those that say and show little. Such people will unleash on you without warning...if you didn't have this book!

Passive aggressive people portray themselves as calm and collected. The ones around me even recite quotes from the Dalai Lama. Don't be fooled, they are suppressing their anger. If you are looking for signs, it is usually found in their opinions. For instance, I write a blog on BurmanBooks.com and Facebook.com about how to deal with fear and adversity. I usually get about 10-14 emails with positive feedback. I will also get about 2–3 from people who disagree. Then I will get 1 from someone who is just angry and trying to disguise it under a disagreement. Their anger is clear when there is no sustenance for their reasoning.

Another example is of a person on my team who passes himself off as someone who likes women. Yet when he speaks of women, he uses derogatory terms like bitch or worse. By hearing his words, you can safely assume that he is angered by women in general. Ask a person like this if he is close to his mother. (People who just say yes are usually saying so out of duty and not because they really believe it.) If he says yes, follow-up with how often he sees or talks to his mother. If you make him feel comfortable, you will get a meaningful, lengthy response. A third question to ask is if he has sisters that he is close to. If he does, ask about the relationship, and if not, ask if he has a girlfriend or wife. This will often lead into a discussion about an 'ex' who left him.

If you ask enough questions, you will find the truth. In the case of my team member, his mother was extremely angry due to the loss of her husbands, so he was sent to be raised by his very angry sister who pushed and beat him during his young years. He never had a female role model. Instead, he endured a mother who gave him up and a sister who ignored and beat him. He unleashed his repressed anger on every woman.

The most difficult part in dealing with passive aggressive people, is taking the time to do it. So take a deep breath. Then, ask the questions and trust that you will find answers.

9. Obesity.

As a hypnotist, you are taught that there is an emotional explanation for everything that happens in the body. Yes, genetics plays a role, but it's the flame we are interested in. You may be more susceptible to a drug addiction than I am, but the addiction itself (drugs, alcohol, gambling) is the symptom of the problem. The same with obesity.

The three factors for weight gain are:

- *Culture:* A person's culture may be very restrictive and ultra conservative, so a person would gain weight to keep themselves from breaking cultural rules.

- *Family:* Family values can cause depression, anxiety and anger should they go against your personal value system. Rebelling without losing the family bond, weight gain is a visual rebuttal.

- *Sex:* If a woman or man has been sexually assaulted in early years, they might express their pain through weight gain as a way of making themselves less attractive to the opposite sex. A client I was treating lost most of her extra weight when we discovered she was raped twice before the age of 14.

BEFORE you get upset, no, I'm not saying because you are overweight you are trying to be unattractive. You may be extremely beautiful. So before you react, read the other two rationalizations and see which one belongs to you. Yes, one of them does. Even myself being overweight, was sexually assaulted in the change room showers of a gym my family belonged to when I was in Grade 2. I didn't think it had any effect on me, but I had so many body issues growing up, and still do, that I know my weight problem can be traced back to the fear of it happening again.

10. Fantasy Makers.

These people are a lot of work to be around, but they are also quite a bit of fun. They have such highs and such lows. When they are high, they laugh, joke and are excited about life. When they have their lows, Oi vey! They cry, are in despair and experience long depression sessions.

Fantasy Makers are people who build high expectations, and when it falls short, they feel defeated. I am still like that, but I watch for it and try to balance it out. I remember getting a green light on a movie at Showtime. It had been packaged by me, which means I represented the author of the book, the screenwriter and was a producer on the movie at the age of 26. After about a week of negotiations, the contract was couriered over to me. I had already spent the money in my mind on a new car, new clothes, coke and hookers (just kidding, sort of). The contract arrived the next day and

before I could open the envelope, I got a call from
Showtime legal affairs department. They told me
not to sign the agreement since the movie was dead.
Dead? Was there anyway I could get a defibrillator
and bring it back to life? No, Showtime's budget had
been cut in half and because my movie was still in
a book form, it would take too long and too much
money to develop. I was so depressed, and because
I had spent the money in my head, it started to
believe I was in debt. This brings on...? Yes, actual
debt, since your body lives what your mind thinks.

The reason for the fantasy in the first place, is
because we don't equalize the hope with reality, we
stay in the warm glow of hope. Hope feels good,
since it sends endorphins all over our body. Reality
introduces the negative side and urges you to think
of a backup plan. Some are very good at doing this,
like my lawyer Bruce. Others need to stay away
from any idea of pain due to past experiences and
feeling powerless.

These personality types are the easiest to sell to,
but are constantly in a state of emotional flux, and
can take a lot of your energy away.

11. Bitter Commiter.

If you have been unsuccessful at love with someone you have had a true connection with, they are or you are a 'Bitter Commiter'. This is a person, usually very attractive, that jumps from one person to another without getting into a real relationship. They act cold and uninterested in any sort of long term possibilities and seem to break up with ease. When we give all of ourselves to this person, we think they are evil for being able to move on with a blink of an eye.

Well, here is the truth about our cold-blooded evil love. They are actually in more pain than you can ever imagine. They have come from abusive relationships, whether physical or emotional. They have been so badly hurt that they have hardened themselves to never go through the process again. However, late at night, when your head is on your pillow, you are unable to lie to yourself. These people truly want to have a loving relationship with you, especially if you open yourself up to them completely. The fear of pain simply overrides their feelings for you, and they will leave.

A common excuse for their behaviour is, "I'm just looking to have fun". "I am not a commitment type of person'. Or the best one is 'I don't see anything wrong with having a lot of sex.' This is funniest when it comes from a woman. They replace emotional fulfillment with physical fulfillment and then make themselves believe that it's the sex they crave, when in fact it's the emotional satiation they yearn for.

The closer you get to them, the sooner they will run. Until they are ready to risk the pain in favour of deep fulfillment. If they never get to that point, they get involved in convenient marriages. This is where they never truly give themselves to the other person, but live out a married lifestyle in order to fit into our cultural system. In a lot of cases the marriage will end, or infidelity occurs, or both. Either way, without the risk of pain, they will never fully appreciate themselves or their partners, and this is one situation where the only healthy thing you can do is leave before you get too emotionally attached.

12. Litter Commiter.

There is also the exact opposite personality. This is the person that will commit to anyone at any point! They litter their lives with commitments to people they haven't spent a lot of time with. They are so full of fear of being alone, that they would rather be in unhealthy relationships than healthy ones. They rarely leave and never cheat. They have to be broken up with and cling like rubber cement paste. They feel they lacked love, and try to make up for it by wanting to be loved by anyone who will have them.

The good part is they are very loyal to you if you get involved with them. Bad news is that they are like the in-laws that never leave.

That was a pretty heavy chapter. Speaking of heavy, I want to share with you my mother's top secret recipe for bran muffins that taste nothing like bran muffins (especially with chocolate chips and walnuts). I am going to be publishing this, so you better like them!

1 cup	All Bran cereal (will keep you regular too!)
1 cup	boiling water
1 cup	sugar
1 cup	butter
2 eggs	
½ quart	buttermilk
2 ½ cup	flour
½ tsp	salt
2 tsp	baking soda
1 cup	chopped walnuts
1 cup	chocolate chips (per muffin...just kidding...well, not really)

Mix together

400 degrees for 20 mins.

CHAPTER THREE

See and Hear

'm hoping that by the end of the book, you will see what you are not being shown, and hear what is not being said. Just because someone laughs, does not mean they are happy. How do they dress? Where do they look when greeting you, directly in the eye or somewhere else? What is their handshake like? What is their body telling you?

Eyes

They truly are the windows to the soul.

This is from the perspective of you looking at the person. So left is your left.

- **Upper right** look is Visual Memory. So when you ask someone about a past memory and to describe what it looked like, they would look up and right.
- **Upper left** if Visual Construction. Therefore

ask someone to see a pink Giraffe skateboarding, they would look upper left.

- **Direct left** would be Auditory Construction. For instance, ask someone to hear the sound of a rabbit singing "My Way" in their head and they would look left.
- **Direct right** would be Auditory Memory. Paris Hilton singing. Enough said.
- **Down left** are feelings or Kinaesthetic. This would be recalling a smell, taste or feeling from the past.
- **Down right** is Internal Auditory or talking to yourself.

Use Cautiously. Some people have twitches or weak eye muscles which may cause what looks like a negative or positive eye movement, but are really just their natural trait. Or, if you have someone like me who is ambidextrous, then I'm using my left and right hand which means it affects the direction in which I access my brain. Culture is another thing that can affect body language and eye movement calculations. In certain cultures it is bad manners to look someone in the eye, and in others, you are to look in the eye at all times.

So, I go by feeling and less logic. When someone looks at me in a certain way, I might get a bit of a shiver and want nothing to do with them. I was approaching a very well known author and speaker about possibly coming to our company. He told me thirty times about the fact that he likes win/win situations. At one point, he looked up at me and back down. I got such a cold feeling I ended the meeting. I later found out that he was not an honest guy.

Remember: Very dark, big retinas indicate bottled anger, or they are on mushrooms!

You will see reactions in split second glimpses. When Will.I.Am responded to the video accusations by Perez Hilton that he beat Hilton up, he responded with his own video stating he did not hit Hilton. After each time he said it, a smirk appeared on his face, not because he did it, but because he was not sad it happened.

When you see someone's eyebrows raise, its showing surprise or confirmation. So, you accuse someone of something they did, and at the point you accuse them, their eyebrows raise, it's showing they are aware of the truth. It can also be at a point of accusation, the person is surprised and holding back. For instance when Bill Clinton was accused of the Monica Lewinsky affair, on the stand he often had his finger in front of his pursed lips and his eyebrows raised. He knew the truth and was withholding it.

■ EXERCISE

Find a partner for this. Since unwanted signs are shown through your eyes, you have to condition yourself to project the right signs. So without using any facial muscles, and therefore not making any facial movements, have them guess what emotion you are portraying through your eyes. Try happiness, sadness and anger. Remember, your face will look the same through all of them since you can't use ANY facial muscles whatsoever.

Keep practicing this until any emotion you want to exude can be guessed by anyone. Great intimidators who say little but process the ability to inject fear into anyone have mastered this.

■ ■ ■ ■ ■ ■ ■ ■ ■ ■ ■ ■ ■ ■ ■

Watch for excess energy

Excess energy gets dissipated into fidgeting, a definite sign that you're nervous or ill at ease. These people will 'unleash' on you in a second's notice if you trigger them. Bouncing legs, tapping with fingers, clicking of pens, chewing on gum, and constantly looking around, all are signs.

Janine Driver suggests you never touch your face, throat, mouth or ears during an interview. The interviewer may think that you're holding something back, typically, the truth. Although this is a false assumption, to try to establish credibility, it's necessary to avoid touching your face.

I was the judge in a talent contest for the East Indian community. It was a national broadcast and the creator of the show said to us that in the final round, he was getting the biggest Bollywood star to appear. Within a second of completing that statement, he scratched the back of his neck. I knew that he had not solidified the deal.

Hands and arms

Clasped hands are a signal that the person is closed off to you. A palm out gesture at shoulder height is an openness and calmness. Over the shoulder is about keeping control over others, like Hitler and the Nazis. People who want to show they mean no harm, will put their palms out and pump their arms slightly at the person threatened. Some people who try and calm a crowd, will put their hands over their heads, palm down, giving the adult to child control gesture. Notice they will not be able to calm the crowd easily. We don't like the idea of being controlled.

To come across as confident, receptive and un-guarded, have your hands open and relaxed on the table. When your body is open, you project trust-worthiness.

Avoid crossing your arms over your chest. It shows that you are close-minded, arrogant, defen-sive or bored and disinterested.

When you see someone rubbing their palms together slowly, run fast! It is a devious gesture. Look for it when people are explaining a deal to you. When you see fast rubbing of the palms, it is excitement and positive.

Finger gestures

Yes, even your fingers say something. When you 'steeple' your fingers, as in finger tips touching looking like a church, it shows confidence and arrogance. There is a pinnacle that you are showing the other person that you sit on.

When someone has their hands clenched palm to palm and fingers in fingers, which is usually a sign of irritation or anxiousness. Presidents who are at a podium being asked questions from the press will sometimes go to that pose if asked a series of questions they don't want to answer.

Hands behind the back

Some people walk around with their hands behind their backs, or holding their wrists. This is a sign of superiority and confidence. The idea of 'nothing can harm me even when I'm not protecting myself' is often true with leaders, royalty or certain celebrities trying to look modest when touring a place or walking with another leader.

As I was putting this all together, I was sitting at a coffee shop waiting for someone that had been delayed. I started to watch this woman get two cups of iced green tea and sit out on the patio. This means she is waiting for someone. She started to scroll and then text on her Blackberry. Being bored, she was in a relaxed position, one foot on the leg of the table and leaning back in the chair with her legs slightly apart.

A few minutes later a tall man with his son and dog came over to the coffee shop. She and the man obviously knew each other and most likely had seen each other around. She got up to walk over and talk to him. The dog jumped on her and she patted him. The son was given some money from his dad, and went in to buy a drink.

She made sure her arms were pulled together in front of her, fore arm to fore arm, and she crossed her feet in front of her. She was making herself as small as she could. She would look down and tilt her head to an angle to look up at him with her eyes, showing her neck. He, being a big guy, had a stance one foot spread slightly in front of the other, and making big gestures with his arms while telling a story. He was making himself bigger.

Remember, I can't hear a word that is being said, only watching through the window. What I knew for sure, was the person she was meeting up with, was in trouble, because she has more of an interest in the man she was flirting with.

The boy came back with his drink and watched his father and the girl talking. He started to play with the dog between the two. He was being threatened by this woman taking his dad's time, he started to separate them. The father took the hint and the girl went back to her table. I thought to myself that maybe I was wrong and there was nothing going on. Just as he passed her, he had his phone out, and after a line exchanged between them, he started to key in her number. Bingo!

About 3 minutes after he left, the boyfriend came, kissed her and sat down. She went back to her original position of foot on the table leg, leaned back position and arms hanging over the sides of the chair. She is the boss of that relationship since he sat legs crossed at the ankles, under the chair, arms on the table leaning in, and more into what she was saying than the other way around. This is a woman whose beauty has probably gotten men to feel insecure, and assume a 'whipped' role in order to keep her which actually bores her. She longs for a big man to take control and be protective.

■ EXERCISE

Shut the sound off on your television and watch politicians, preachers and journalists. It is amazing to see how clearly their bodies are rejecting things they are saying. Reflect upon the body language of President Obama, for instance, when he spoke to Senator McCain. He looked off for a split second before answering him as if annoyed, and he even used his middle finger to scratch his forehead.

Now that you hear their body, you can listen to their voice. Did it match your assumptions?

■ ■ ■ ■ ■ ■ ■ ■ ■ ■ ■ ■ ■ ■

When I give lectures on hypnosis, I say that we talk 'at' people more than we talk 'to' people. Have the other person do all the talking. Human nature makes it so we love to talk about ourselves. One of the best interviewers on television is Barbara Walters, because she listens more than she talks. She lets the person she's interviewing tell her what her next question should be. If you give them a chance, people will reveal their personality but also, how they process information.

We process information one of three ways: audibly, visually or aesthetically.

You can tell by their use of words how they process information. For instance, if they use 'I felt' or 'I was shocked' or 'was hurt', they are aesthetic thinkers. Best move you can make is showing effort and thoughtfulness in details. For example, have a candlelight dinner. Cook the dinner and if possible give the mood a very romantic feel (soft music). If they employ 'I saw' or 'I wore' or 'It looked like' more often, they are visual. Visual thinkers love expensive gifts. They will also notice details, so don't wear the same shirt two days in a row! Audible thinkers will say 'I heard' or 'She sounded like' or 'all you could hear'. A perfect thing for audible thinkers would be a unique CD, tickets to a concert or orchestral performance.

■ EXERCISE

Consider the following examples and attempt to categorize them correctly:

Example 1: A woman complains about a date's blabbering. She describes how turned off she was, even how she raised the volume on the stereo to quiet his incessant talking.

Example 2: A baker who describes the difference between French bread and Italian bread by the cut on the top and how the cut changes the look, but not the test or texture.

Example 3: A woman describes being with her husband on a Sunday evening watching movies, cuddled in his arms on the sofa, relaxed and stress-free before the new week begins.

Hopefully you correctly identified the first person as someone who processes information audibly, the second visually, and the third aesthetically. If a person offers a similar story to these examples, they are giving you a manual to their processing methods. We can alter perception of motivation by

understanding the way the brain processes information. Start talking to people in general, whether
you know them or not, and see how quickly you can
detect how their brain processes and which
methodology would best be used to communicate
with them.

Remember we ALL have three processing
avenues (unless you are blind or deaf), so just
because someone happens to say 'I heard', doesn't
necessarily make them audible. If you can't figure it
out, revert to aesthetic. We all 'feel'. Which is why
when I'm giving a lecture to a large crowd, I always
use aesthetic words to communicate to the majority.

■ ■ ■ ■ ■ ■ ■ ■ ■ ■ ■ ■ ■ ■

....

CHAPTER FOUR

You know it's a lie when...

The human body is a natural lie detector. The only people this does not apply to are psychopaths or sociopaths. Other than that, our bodies react to our thoughts. Some of the signs will occur in 1/8th of a second, but they are there. The subconscious and conscious are constantly battling. The subconscious is a child that is very open and does or says things, independent of what our conscious mind wants to communicate. Tell someone a lie. Make a conscious effort NOT to give away any signs. You will feel the smallest sign force itself out like swallowing hard, a twitch, or even more extreme, sweating. Even though your conscious mind will verbalize whatever lie you want to tell, your subconscious will verbalize guilt.

The first thing to look for in spotting a lie, are contradictions. For instance, a person who lies may not avoid eye contact with you! They may stare you straight in the face. The difference between a stare of interest and a stare of confrontation is in the pupils. If the pupils are constricted, they are getting confrontational. They will shift their body away from you ever so slightly, and they will scratch their ear, nose, neck or head. They may even frown when they make a statement. 'I like seeing you' may be followed by a very quick smirk. No, this is not 'just an itch', or a regular facial movement, these are tell-tale signs.

Specific Lie Indicators

The hand covers the mouth even slightly. It might only be one finger, but it is the body rejecting the words that are coming out. We made the Clinton observation in the last chapter.

- **Extending blinking.** They will blink longer than that a normal blink or they will be blinking rapidly. Look at how Madonna answers certain questions during interviews. Based on her answers, some of them come with enough blinking to cause a workout sweat!
- When you see the **'Shh' gestures** being used by an adult to another adult, that is something

that shouldn't come out of their mouth. This is subconscious reflecting back as a child to when your parents gave you that sign to keep quiet.

- **A split second touching of the nose.** I was being interviewed by a radio DJ who kept asking about this book. She said that she is just very busy and therefore has no time for a relationship. I told her as she scratched her nose that she had experienced a very bad break up and kept herself busy to avoid getting attached again. She stuttered and moved to another question laughing nervously.

- **The neck touch** on the back of the neck or the side.

- **The eye rub** indicates not wanting to see the truth or embarrassment.

- **The ear tug** is validation as a satisfactory lie to themselves.

- **The collar pull** is discomfort from telling a lie. In my book, *Do Everything They Tell You Not To Do,* I describe Shoshanna Lonstien, the girl of my dreams, modeling her lingerie designs by placing them in front of her and asking me what I thought of them. I go on to write about how I responded with a simple 'nice', and then tried to unbutton my collar, which led to me pulling my button right off. Obviously, I thought it was more than just 'nice' and she laughed.

Regardless of the object used, such as fingers, cigarettes, or pens, touching the lips or mouth is an attempt to feel more secure. Contact with the lips recalls the comfort of breastfeeding.

Delayed reactions are clear indicators of a lie. For instance, I love watching people open gifts. They will say they love it and stare at it for about a second, before finally following with a smile. Sometimes I give a bad gift just to see if the person is honest. If you give them something they don't really like, see the smile without wrinkles, see the stare at the gift, and then see how they thank you. It will be with a hug that involves a pat on your back, or a handshake that is quick, and then a stare back at the gift. If you add in 'Now don't you go and give it to someone else!" see the eyebrows raise and the uncomfortable laugh showing discomfort and realization that their body had already planned on doing that.

Also, pay attention to objects placed between

you and the other person. They may have a book, toy or even pen that they will fidget with. This is a way of subconsciously putting space between you and them, in order to protect themselves. I remember confronting a woman on her drug addiction in a restaurant. She was so embarrassed that she looked down and smiled subtly and had the drink menu standing up and was fidgeting with it like she was semi-reading it. Also in the previous chapter I told you about my friend and I speaking about his ex-wife.

Warning: Don't come to quick conclusions until you have studied the person for at least a minute to see if they have a natural twitch, dry skin or back injury that deviates from the norm.

■ EXERCISE

You can do this out loud or internally. Look at yourself in the mirror. See at least up to your waist. Now
with belief, tell yourself a lie. State your name is
'Bob' for all that matters (unless your name is really
Bob). Stare for 3 seconds.

Now, you did something as you said it, even if it
was said internally. What was it? Some of you swal-
lowed, some of you twitched and some of you has
a scratch on your neck or cheek. Some of you had a
completely different tell sign.

Even when you know you are going to say a lie,
your sub-conscious will still reject it.

■ ■ ■ ■ ■ ■ ■ ■ ■ ■ ■ ■ ■ ■

CHAPTER FIVE

You know they are into you when. . .

This is fun. It is amazing how men get lazy once we have found our woman. But until then, these are the signs that will help you read your date, whether male or female.

A man instinctively needs to be the bigger one and in control. We are the protectors and we do things unconsciously to prove that.

For instance:

A man will stretch and let out a groan almost as a sign of power and strength. Lions, apes and birds do the same thing.

He may put his hands on his belt, or his hand may rest near his crotch or on his upper thigh. These are signs of...well, you can figure that part out.

Men usually sit with their legs apart. This isn't just because we are lazy and it feels comfortable, it's also being romantic, in an ape-man sort of way.

He will stand close to the woman and may put her against a wall to show protection and 'guarding' over her. Women play to that instinctively.

A woman usually does the following:

Will play with her hair to show she is very feminine and wants him to see how pretty she is (unless she has lice).

She will make herself smaller. Women buy the smallest shoe they can fit on their feet, the clothing that most accentuates their most feminine physical traits and will stand with her arms tucked into her body slightly to show a demure, soft image. When a couple is getting romantic, he will bring her into his chest, and she will tuck her arms into her chest while he holds her. This is the dominant/ submissive roles being played out.

A woman will also expose or bring attention to her neck and lean into the table to show undivided interest. You might actually see their heads tip to the side slightly just to fully expose their neck. This also gives you the side of the neck they are most sensitive on, so if you get to a romantic stage, you can stroke her favourite side of her neck very gently with your finger tips. Again, a romantic stage, not when your mom asks you to take out the garbage. Not cool.

Finally, they're into you when...

- The eyes widen slightly and the eyebrows go up, even a millimetre. I was not subtle as a teenager, so I would literally stare into a girl's eyes to see if her pupils would dilate when she was talking to me. If someone is excited or stimulated, their eyes dilate up to 3 times their original size.
- If she 'looks up' slightly and her eyes have to go up to see yours, it is submissive and fragile and looking for protection from you.
- The slight pouting of the lips, almost like a kiss.
- If the person is hesitating leaving a room, inching closer to leaving, but slightly looking back to see where you are and if you are following.
- A true smile is on display when laugh lines are displayed around the cheeks and eyes. This one is a little difficult with the invention of Botox, but for those who still remain pure, any smile that does not process laugh lines is not a genuine smile.

A couple's hitting it off when…

They start to mirror each other. For instance, if he puts his head on his hand while leaning on the table, she does the same. If he laughs, she will as well. There will be 'accidental' or 'joking' touching going on. If he says something funny she may laugh and give him a bit of a push or hit on his arm playfully. While walking, their hands may touch once or twice. She may even rub her chest against his arm.

CHAPTER SIX

You know where you stand in negotiations when. . .

- Head tilted up slightly, and chin forward is a sign of defiance or superiority. This person wants you to know they are bigger and more powerful than you.
- If the legs of the person are on a 45 degree angle, it means they are not really comfortable with you and their legs want to walk out the door.
- If they have crossed their ankles, usually under their chair, they are getting irritated or anxious.
- If a man crosses his leg over his lap, he is presenting a free-spirited but powerful image. However, a woman will not do this even if she is projecting the same image, since it will send a sexual signal. A woman will generally cross

one leg over the other. This is a demure, sophis-
ticated and intelligent look.

- The subtle head movement from side to side
  before you finish your sentence means the person is rejecting your idea.

I f you hug someone and they pat your back, they
are not comfortable with the hug and want out.

When someone removes their glasses to
clean them unnecessarily or the cleaning of dirt off
the pants unnecessarily is a sign the person is
rejecting your idea and trying to distract themselves
from having to hear any more of it. I was in a pitch
meeting at the studio and as I told the executive
about the script concept, he kept flicking a piece of
lint off his shirt. I stopped talking about the script
and started to ask him about his son who was
pictured on his desk starting baseball. Needless to
say the movie wasn't made.

Leaning back, sometimes with a foot on a table
or chair and a slight laziness in their speaking pattern is a sign they are disinterested and unengaged.

For example, during a scandal on Jon and Kate
Plus 8, in which Jon allegedly had an affair with a
woman, the reality show profiled both sides. When

Jon spoke, he was laid back, sleepy, and his feet were on a stool. He was completely unengaged over something as important as his marriage falling apart. Kate on the other hand was sitting at the edge of the sofa, tearing and slightly leaning elbows which were placed on her lap to show she was interested in the conversation.

She is contained but ready to explode and he is showing little interest because he is ready to explode. The way two personalities, aggressive and passive, deal with frustration and anger.

If you feel that your speech, interview or introduction is not going well and you are seeing negative results in their body language, change it simply by making physical adjustments. For instance, move a few feet to the other side, make a sudden arm gesture or when you come to a strong point, be quiet before strongly delivering your key point with a little raise in your volume.

CASE STUDY

Read the following scene. At the end, make an evaluation as to what I should do. The scene is a true story and I was involved.

It was a very hot summer's day. Driving on the highway, the cars were forced to exit by the police. Being that all the cars on the highway were now using the city streets, there was a traffic jam. Adding to the heat, this was really frustrating.

As the cars eased forward slowly, we came across a park with hundreds of people starting across the street and pointing cameras. As I looked in the same direction, I saw a man standing over the bridge railing threatening to jump off the bridge onto the highway below. There were police everywhere and two cops were yelling back and forth.

The suicide threat was a scruffy man in his late 20s and his khaki coloured 'bomber pants' were slightly stained in the front probably from holding the rail of the bridge. His T-shirt was that of a motorcycle company. He was screaming with his chin cocked forward but his body was leaning back over the 40 foot drop.

The police had surrounded him in semi-circle, but were keeping a safe distance from him. A couple had their hands on their sides, not quite on their guns. The wannabe jumper then started to shout orders while flailing his right arm around.

I had two choices:

(A) I could use my experienced to create a rapport and talk him down.

(B) Or, I could go home.

Read through the case again to figure out what I should / did do.

ANSWER:

It was too hot and I wanted to get home to my air conditioning.

The reason I could leave the scene comfortably was because:

- chin cocked shows arrogance as he 'looked down on the police' (like I do when I get speeding tickets)
- yelling at the cops shows room for negotiation.
- arms flailing in front of a large crowd shows he is seeking attention.

Because he is interacting and enjoying the attention, there is room for negotiation. He obviously shows contempt for the cops so he has most likely been in trouble before and is showing off his superiority over them.

Finally, he picked a spot with a 40 foot drop. He may fall, but only to break a bone, but hard to die. If he was serious, he wouldn't want a lot of attention, and he would be experiencing shame. He would pick a higher place to jump from to guarantee death, and he wouldn't have time to talk, he would be focused on jumping.

I went home.

CHAPTER 7

Assault victims and the after effects

People who have been molested, assaulted, abused or raped are usually emotionally scarred. They feel towards certain people the way you would feel if you shut the car door on your finger. You are very careful when closing the door after that because it would remind you of the time you screamed in pain.

When we discuss these people who have experienced something tragic like that, the signs are very important to read. Depending on their value system, the age it happened, and the situation that took place, it will be acted out differently. However, they will ALWAYS act it out. Their bodies are in such pain, fear and anger, it expresses itself differently for everyone.

For instance a girl I went to high school with was considered if not the prettiest, than one of the prettiest in school. All the boys wanted to be with

her and she looked like she probably had the greatest life ever! The truth was confessed to me years
later when she told me about the fact that the other
girls hated her and due to jealousy, tortured her
emotionally and sometimes physically. She went
on to tell me that her parents had a strict curfew so
she wasn't able to go out at night like most high
schoolers do, and the boys all just wanted to sleep
with her, which made her paranoid about men.
The after effects of this shocking revelation have
developed her into a person that can go from 0-100
on the temper scale with only a one word trigger!
She can get irate if you question her or if she feels
pressured in any way. This is all due to the fact she
has suppressed all the hostility from her past and it
shows itself as a 'girl with a huge temper'. It really
doesn't matter if the incident happened in high
school, home, or in a relationship, anyone with a
hair trigger temper is really lashing out at anything
that can remind them of the past. We usually pass
it off as someone difficult to work with or worse
'Bitch' under our breath, but really they are in pain
and trying their best to run away from it.

In the following examples, you have to imagine
what the person has gone through and then pick

your words to avoid confrontation. An example is a person I know who courageously survived cancer twice. She is a model, so on top of having her hair fall out, she was not able to work. One day I said to her "Life is too short and we should live it up". I didn't say it to her directly, just out loud and in general. She got so upset at me and asked me what I meant by that. She went on to tell me I have no idea what I'm talking about and should stop judging her! Literally I couldn't even put the slice of pizza in my mouth. I was just frozen from her reaction towards a general statement. When she left and I had time to review the conversation in my head, I realized her lashing out was more at herself and the idea she has confronted death twice and therefore knows more than anyone how short life is. Human error, but one I can avoid next time.

Here are some scenarios that prior trauma could act itself out:

Lesbians, Clubbers and Condoms

I have some friends that are gay and I find it interesting to analyze my interactions with them. In my research of gay relationships I have come to the conclusion that 83% of gay men are truly born gay, and surprisingly only 37% of gay women are truly born gay (from the body language and verbiage when asked questions and daily lifestyle habits). One research according to The International Lesbian Information Service states 50% of women have had lesbian experiences and feelings! When I say 'born gay', I'm referring to such persons that are only attracted to the same sex and have never been interested or attracted to the opposite sex. I said this to a gay friend of mine and he laughed so hard because apparently this is an ongoing joke in the gay community.

Why then are there so many women stating they are lesbians when they aren't? In my opinion these statistics are a result of emotional trauma. They truly believe they are attracted to women, but the reason they are is different than the women actually born as lesbians. I had dinner with a friend of mine who is a lesbian for over 15 years now, and I get the impression from our conversations that she needs to prove to me that she is in fact gay. The funny part is that she always shows me her 'girlie' side, as in she likes me to drive her car to the restaurant or if she pays for dinner, and will give me the money to look like I'm paying. If it was a random girl you would meet on the street, you would say she was attracted to me (or so my friends and parents seemed to think).

When we had dinner together, she and I got into a heated discussion as I challenged her on her lifestyle. After emotions ran high, she blurted out that her father tried to sleep with her. She went on to say that she had dated men in the past, but she didn't feel she was treated well. She then retracted that when I quoted her, and she said she was treated extremely well. Sounds confusing? Well now you are getting a glimpse of how confused she is in her mind.

The idea of running to another woman is like nourishment to another woman's soul. She needs to be lightly touched, kissed and caressed, with no reservations because she knows she isn't going to have her body ravaged by an imposing or domineering man. In a sense, she is looking for companionship. She feels secure and non-threatened in the relationship.

This friend also feels the need to only go after women who are straight in an attempt to convince them that they haven't yet gotten in touch with their 'lesbian' side. She tried this on my cousin, who came and told me there was no way she was a lesbian. And getting back to an earlier lesson of preaching what you learn, my friend feels the need to express to everyone that she is a lesbian. It's almost like her calling card. Without being one, who is she?

The reason is when her father tried to sleep with her, her identity was taken away. Everyone needs an identity, and she gets the most attention out of being a lesbian. Another big clue is their choice in women partners. My friend will openly admit she can only go out with other hot girls. This is to be noticed, and again, goes to identity.

I have another woman I know who claims to be a lesbian, and it's the same story, but from a traumatic rape when she was 13. She felt she needed to run from any resemblance to that night by escaping with other women. Both of the women in my examples are not happy. They don't have a relationship with anyone, and they feel isolated in their worlds, so they work constantly. They are in pain.

Now, there are those naturally attracted only to women, one of whom worked for my parents. She had this very natural 'male' energy about her, even though not all lesbians are like that. But importantly it wasn't a 'put on' or forced. Scientists have been working for years on trying to see why this is, and if it comes from a gene or another reason, but the answer is not the point of this book.

Don't fall for the girls in clubs that kiss other girls. This is an act of desperation to capture male attention in most cases. If they really are more interested in women, and were not doing it for attention purposes, they would go to gay clubs where they will not be bothered or stared at. Those girls carry condoms, and not because they make better balloons!

The gay men are similar. The ones who are born gay know it at an early age. They may date girls in high school to fit in, but a lot of the ones who become gay are emotionally or physically abused by their fathers. They have become so afraid of the alpha male types, they completely rebel and become involved with another man. Why not a gentle woman? Because the abuse has taken them into a shell and they take on a more feminine, nurturing type of personality to give what they were never given.

Remember, not all men who are abused wake

up and become gay. This is only with the small percentage that have become over time attracted to males.

The Slut Phenomenon

"Did you see the girl at that bar last night? Holy cow, she had her boobs pushed almost out of her bikini top and she looked like she was going to make out with that dude any second!" Words all young men have stated to each other at one point or another. But the question is, was she really as easy as she looked?

A rule you learn in your late teen years or early 20's is you never go for the hot girl looking the most provocative, you almost always go for her quiet friend just behind her that is not getting any attention. Of course, I wouldn't know if that's true, since I never did the one night stand thing.

A woman who has been sexually assaulted or abused physically or emotionally will sometimes act out for the constant need of attention by males. She will get their attention by sleeping with them or by dressing provocatively. For us to properly analyze this, we need to go back to the father/ daughter relationship. The group of girls I know that have a healthy respect for themselves, and are in the 28–34 age group, have never slept with more than 6 people. They told me they believed it was because of their father being so strict with them and wanting to know where they were at all times. One told me that as much as she hated him at the time for always intruding in her life, she looks back and thanks God. Another one told me her father gave her all the latitude it the world, and only gave her advice when she asked, but always listened to her. She said that by him not passing judgment, she felt that she had to earn his respect.

When I look at the girls I have dated in my past, almost all of them have had very stern and unemotional fathers. He was rarely around, infrequently asked them where they were going or with whom, and never really hugged or kissed them. This caused a need for the girls to get the male attention they were so thirsty for. Even though the male attention they get from sleeping around or flirting with guys is insincere and unhealthy, it's still male attention at the end of the day. They feel attractive, loved and feminine for even just a few minutes. I'm thinking they need a dominant male figure which would answer their attraction to me, and they are extremely accommodating to my controlled lifestyle.

A male that has been abused as a child can act out as homophobic, aggressive, angry and in severe cases a rapist or abuser. Again, they feel so much rage inside for what happened to them, they express it through anger to other people. Almost like the person has to feel their pain.

A former trainer of mine has a body of a Gladiator, and if he isn't in jail, he's in street fights or training for the UFC. He is yearning to be loved, but is also so trapped by his anger, he has only physical exertion to release his feelings temporarily.

The heir to a grocery chain is not only beautiful, talented and very classy looking, she is also very approachable. But if you look into her eyes, they don't change expression even though she might smile or laugh. She is very distant with men, and will usually stay in a relationship for a short time before moving on. Her choice of man is the model look, and in great physical shape. This is important because what it means when you see a very pretty girl with a mode-looking man, it means there is a lot of insecurity in herself and how she is seen in society. She is also in lust, because love is too painful to experience. She is also into keeping control, therefore when the time to leave comes, she is not bothered too much by it. She is the type to ask a man to come over for sex, but have him leave immediately afterwards, not because she misses sex, but because she has juxtaposed sex with the feeling of temporary security and affection. You will never be able to get involved with a person like this if you are interested in long term, until the person wants to deal with their emotional pain and anger towards men. Men can also act this way if they have been hurt by a woman from their past and will act it out by dating only stunning women that they can have control over and show to society how in demand they are.

Cult Followers

Cults are successful because they give a person what they most need: security, sense of belonging and love.

A large percentage of people who I have worked with and end up getting caught up to a point of obsession in the self help world, and even start speaking like they are born from the loins of 'Princess Love'. This new world to them becomes their universe. They feel they must advertise it, push it on others and spend all of their time immersed in it.

I'm not saying he is, but Tom Cruise-type personalities usually come from abusive fathers and revert to clubs, societies or religions that can give them emotional nourishment. Again, not saying that he is or isn't. The positive part is that they really have good intentions. They want the rest of the world to feel as great as they do, but their insecurities also participate in them needing to feel that they are not alone in this new found 'enlightenment'.

S & M

I found out that a person I know went out with a girl I also know, and apparently he likes to have his face slapped and penis stomped on. It so happens this is what occurs on all my dates, even though I don't like it. I was treating a single mother who was raped on her birthday by the football quarterback and even though states she has resolved those issues, love to be photographed hogtied and whipped. Again, reminding me of my prom night in high school. Getting back to her, she is showing how she feels about herself. There is humiliation and degradation still in her psyche. She also loves to dominate men in bed, showing anger towards the opposite sex.

Some would judge her as being strange or crazy, but really she is expressing what is inside her subconscious. In fact I know many adult film stars that retire because they can't take it anymore. They literally feel so denigrated that they throw in the towel hoping to finally rid themselves of that feeling.

Now again, I will state that these are broad strokes and general symptoms. We can do a whole book on each symptom in detail. I just want you to recognize the signs.

CASE STUDY

All the following women are 28 years old and have been assaulted. Pick which woman has most probably been assaulted by 12 years old and remember to use not only instinct, but the clues that seem insignificant.

Girl 1:
Very friendly, very open minded to learning about other cultures and foods. She is like an open book and talks to everyone. She has a close tight pact with a few girls, but well known in the charity and social conscious world. She comes from an educated background and close family. She carries a small air horn, and keeps her purse under her arm. She also likes to be walked to a garage parking lot with someone else, and gets a little nervous when walking alone at night and a group of men are behind her. She will speed up to a brisk walk. She dates educated and successful men, but more turned on my intellectual abilities rather than materialistic trophies. Tough father who is

very successful and a stay at home mother who is very nurturing.

Girl 2:

A club girl, meaning she is always at nightclubs dancing and drinking all night long. She has a boring retail job, and tells herself she is going to quit, but never does. She will make out with guys, and if on a first date, can be convinced to give oral sex. Most of her facebook pictures show her laughing wildly with her friends and mostly in nightclubs. She is friendly and always welcomes new people to her social life. She dresses seductively in tight clothing with little exposure. She has bouts of emotional highs and lows, and when depressed, will cry alone in her room and then go out to party as hard as she can. Drugs do sometimes get used at clubs, and it's usually ecstasy, but sometimes cocaine. Her parents are very good to her but have little control over her. Her mother is soft spoken, as is her father, and they do spend some evenings together every week.

Girl 3:
Severely overweight. Dresses very provocatively and usually smiles without showing her teeth or crow's feet. She is quiet but can get very loud and physical when provoked. She also goes to night-clubs a lot and loves the attention from guys, but will only go home with the one that plays it cool and distant. She smokes a lot of pot, and will sometimes compete with the boys to see who can drink the most alcohol. She likes Ultimate Fighting, Indy cars and motorcycles. She is alone since she has few friends, and even they are more of close acquaintances. She has a small dog and has little to do with her parents. Her father is a blue collar worker who has shift work, and mother is a secretary at a large corporation.

ANSWER:

Girl 3 is the one who has most probably been assaulted by the age of 12. In some cases, the memory has been so far repressed, they have forgotten it, and in others, they feel it was so insignificant that it has nothing to do with them. Our Girl uses sex to attract men, and is so angry in life that she is unable to show happiness and reacts to the smallest situation. It is easy to tell from her pictures that she is unhappy by the smile she shows in all of them. The way she dresses shows she is trying to attract male attention through the only way she knows how, and her sleeping around and her marijuana use is to deaden the sadness.

Girl 2 was assaulted, but probably from being drunk or high and ending up in a bad situation. She is always in a group not only because she feels lonely, but also because it will avoid the same situation from repeating itself. Her anger, depression and need for male attention most likely comes from the fact her father is more of a female role player in the household since he is very soft spoken, doesn't show protectiveness towards her and she feels inside she is not loved by him, but thinks that she is logically. A lot of females who come and see me are usually in my chair because they have felt something lacking in their relationship with their father from a young age. Her dresses seductively but not trying to look like a prostitute is to get her father's attention and yet keep what little dignity she has left in hopes her father will question her or show some authority as she feels a father should.

Girl 1 was most likely felt up at in a public place or maybe victim of theft at knife point. She is protective of her surroundings, but is trying less to be a target. Due to her strong family support system, she has not let it change her psyche that much, however she takes more precautions to not allow it to happen again.

CHAPTER 8

Self Sabotage

Edmund Bergler wrote about 'Pleasure in Displeasure Syndrome'. We will get into it in the second section as well, but it is so important to not only see the signs in others, but in yourself. I hated the fact that for so long I was struggling to attain success in my early 20's, and yet nothing was happening. I wrote in my last book, *Do Everything They Tell You Not To Do*, that I went through depression. Partying all night and sleeping all day because I just wasn't seeing results in my career. The reason came to me after studying this subject. It's called Self Sabotage, and it's about the sub-conscious part of the brain not believing it is ready or worthy of success. Some do it in their relationships and others at work.

To illustrate what your body is doing to you, the left front and right tires on your car are in drive gear, while the left side of your front and rear tires are in reverse. The car isn't going even a centimetre forward, until it finally breaks and dies.

I have had the experience of working with some well known people in my life so far. One of them was a former movie theatre magnate who we will call Darth, since his evilness reminded me of Darth Vader. Darth was brilliant. He had a mind so creative, he could turn shit into Shinola. The problem was Darth developed a physical ailment when he was young which made him an outsider. He was in serious pain all his life from the ailment and was probably bullied. His revenge was to revolutionize the film exhibition/distribution market. His demise? His greed.

He then returned forming a live theatre company with magnificent set designs, fantastic live shows and major actors starring. His demise? His greed.

He was always making good money from his ventures, in fact millions of dollars. He was in the headlines constantly and he was playing with the top players in Hollywood. His sub-conscious still made him feel like he was the abnormal kid who wasn't liked. It pointed out the fact that he will never fit into society and will never truly be liked for who he is and not how much he has. He's on trial for allegedly stealing from his company.

The funny thing about Darth is that I really liked him when we went out for lunch. He took me to a deli and we talked about life and his history. I was producing a debate style show for CBC Newsworld and thought Darth would be a great person to have on the show to debate a very well known civil rights lawyer. When we were just about to close, Darth, at the last second, demanded a huge fee, one that surpassed the budget of the show.

Darth had a great opportunity to show himself in front of the public as a well spoken and well educated guy. Instead, greed, really the front for his insecurities of not fitting in, took over and he killed his own deal.

I had a company that was bought out by a venture capitalist. The silent partner of the firm was a very wealthy heir to a candy fortune. He put about $5 million into the firm and after I left, I found out he never got a penny back. His partner had moved on to another idea, pulling the plug on the company and therefore stated he didn't owe any money. Would you be angry? The heir still talks to the partner and is upset about the money, but won't do anything to recover it. Ok, maybe $5 million isn't going to jeopardize his world, but still, to keep in contact with the person that stiffed you? I remember starting my company and a measly $200,000, and was laughed at when I asked him for it. It wasn't the spending of the money that was the problem he told me, it was the fact he wouldn't make much back on a $200,000 investment. So to lose $5 million on a douche bag was more of a risk and 'gambler's rush', but to help a young person start their life was not possible.

It's funny because the amount of self-sabotage in that style of thinking surpasses Donald Trump liking his own hair style. It's perplexing! However the heir will tell you on his own that he suffers from it every day. He was taught as a kid how to make money. He was told you don't do something unless it makes money. This is why you get multi-millionaires that can't help someone out for a few thousand dollars but will lose millions on yachts, horses or travelling the world. They do it because in their minds, they are not worthy of what they have. If they inherited it, or they happen to make it big from an invention, they don't understand it, and they feel guilt from it.

I break the balls (mind the expression) of a media executive who is very powerful and very rich. He has no kids, no wife and no life. He is totally loyal to his shareholders, whom would replace him in 3 minutes tomorrow, if he didn't continue doing his job. The amount of phone calls would be reduced from 60 a day to about 4. He leaves nothing behind. All the shows, the stations and the deals will be forgotten 20 years from now. His life is a turmoil of guilt, sadness, power and image. For him to green light a show, put something into development or put an interview on one of his stations can be done in a heartbeat, but yet, does not happen. Not because it isn't right or favours are never done in Hollywood, but because he suffers from self sabotage in getting a personal life. In connecting with another human being can be a painful experience for him. He chooses to live his life fully immersed in work to avoid the idea of pain or betrayal or rejection from an experience in his past.

A girl I was sort of dating, would get very close to me, and then pull back for weeks. Then again, she would come forward and leave. She would use the excuses of being busy, but really it was her way

of protecting herself and sabotaging the relationship. In fact, just after I submitted my first draft of
this book, we had dinner and she told me about
her friend who was being led on by a guy that her
friend liked, and cried all night on the phone with
her. Her response to me was "I would never let a
guy do that to me!" From the words she uses, you
can understand her actions.

My lawyer had a client, an aesthetician, that he
defended in a civil suit against a person who
suffered a hair removal injury that took place on a
client of hers. Bruce went against the odds and got
the woman off with just a slap on the wrist. She
repaid him by writing post dated cheques, and
when it came time to cash them, she would call
him to tell him not to, due to lack of funds. The
reason for lack of funds? She was vacationing in
Hawaii or Paris. This is the personality that no
matter how good you are to them, they will do
something to destroy it under the façade of being
selfish. They are really scared of having people be
good to them, only to let them down.

A last example of self sabotage are those that
suffer from Homo-Masochism which is telling
themselves and believing they really want it badly,

but still work against themselves. A great example would be Lindsay Lohan. She had the greatest career ever and could do no wrong! She was not only a good actress but also picked great roles. In fact, if she had 2 bad movies in a row, Hollywood would have forgiven her and still paid her big bucks.

The problem was that Lindsay felt the pressure of Hollywood, the paparazzi and the massive fortune she was building at a young age. She looked at how her fame and money stirred hatred between the father and mother and its toll on the family. So, her sub-conscious decided that if she lost the fame, all would go back to normal. All of her actions were not consciously to lose all she had built, but she was not showing up to sets on time, she was turning down good roles and taking on bad ones. She finally dug her own grave and now she is just a great story for the tabloids.

Being Too Nice

We love having those people that will bend over backwards to please us. It's true, even though we may feel a little guilty that they put much more into you than you do into them. What makes them want to over exceed generosity comes from the insecurity of needing to be liked. My mother is one of those people. If you were to walk into the house and say you liked the sofa, she would give it to you. My father or I would be left with the responsibility of having to haul it out, but she doesn't care about that, she only wants the person to think she is nice and generous. It sucked to have nice toys, because the minute another kid liked it, it was taken from me and given to them. I'm thinking I was abused.

The great thing about having these people around is that they are loyal and almost always happy. Again, it comes down to the idea that if they were to show they were in a bad mood or needed to vent, you wouldn't care or think they are a nuisance and leave them. Conrad Black, whom I feel loyal to since he helped pay for my college education, was going through his court hearings over corporate fraud. I had written to him several times stating he should stop answering every question the media asks. He was not able to say "No comment". He wanted so badly to be liked by the public since he had been portrayed as the perfect villain. His stature, cold look and dark eyes didn't help him at all, but on top of that between he charges and his mono-linguistic style, he was made to look evil. I could see right away that by him answering all questions the media asked, he was trying to show his side, but also that he wasn't bad at all and quite approachable. Nope. The more he answered, the more the media played him like a violin, and at the end of the day, he was convicted and sentenced.

The idea of being nice is great. The idea of losing one's self to be liked isn't. A background for people like that is usually feeling like they don't fit in at school, with the neighbourhood kids or are very self-conscious. One female friend of mine was almost in tears when I told her she was the 'emotional garbage can' of her friends. I know it sounds harsh, but I wanted her to clearly see how that was and hopefully stop it. She wanted so badly to be liked, so she stopped voicing things that bothered her and simply repressed it since in her mind she was not important enough for people to take time and listen. After we had that conversation, one of her friend's dated her ex-boyfriend without telling her, and she unleashed on her friend with the fury of the Trojan army! I was quite proud of her for finally stating her disappointment in someone else without the insecurity of whether or not she will be liked after that.

Her insecurity might come from the fact she is exceptionally tall and must have felt awkward in school since most boys are not her height. Feeling like she can be the support system to others might have made her feel that is the way to fit in and get people to ignore how she stands out in a crowd. She is very pretty and has a sincere laugh with a hug that grabs you and holds you tightly, she really needs to just understand that her personality alone is all that she needs to fit in. From there, a person can start to create more self-esteem and draw boundaries.

Reaching Your Goal

I t doesn't matter who or what you are going up against, there is a strategy for getting what you want. Anyone who is successful, got there by not giving up, but also walked in with a predetermined idea of what they wanted and filled in the gaps with strategy like the ones in this book. This works for any scenario. If you think it through, you will walk in with the advantage, whether business or professional.

In the first section you learned to:

- Determine your desired outcome.
- Look at the person's traits (clothing, etc...) and sum them up in your head. You might not be able to get their favourite colour, but you should know the broad strokes.
- Assess objects and environments. Always take a quick look around and see if your assumptions about their personality match their choices in decor.
- Read their body language to gage where they are mentally and emotionally.

In this section, you will learn to:

- Mirror to establish a rapport.
- Not preach.
- Identify Addiction.
- Strive for Balance.
- Aim for Success.
- Recognize No is Yes.
- Choose your Unknown Heaven over your Known Hell.

Introduction

Intention is everything. Intention walks in the door $1/4$ second before you do. The feeling you process inside is what comes through your eyes. For example, have you ever had a thought about something that made you mad, anxious or sad, and everyone else around you looked at you and asked if you were alright? A feeling internally gets expressed externally before a word is exchanged. If you are walking into a room, think of something cheerful, motivating or funny. You will immediately put your audience at ease.

Get What You Want

CHAPTER ONE

Mirroring to establish rapport

Creating rapport is creating a connection between you and the other person. The ONLY way to get people to hear you or do as you ask, is through rapport. I always like to say out loud when I'm feeling resistance: 'We both have the same goal'. When the editor of this book, Jean, was feeling uncomfortable telling me the uncensored truth, I needed to establish rapport with her to get her defences lowered. So I said 'We both are trying to make this book the best it can be. So no matter what you tell me, it's to better the book'. Once that was said, her comfort level rose and she cut 9000 words. Ouch. (I snuck this line in AFTER she edited the entire book). You can also create rapport through a fondness for sports, kids, jobs, or anything that is the same in the other person. Rapport can be built within 4 seconds to 1 minute.

NLP founders, Bandler and Grinder, created the technique called mirroring. If the person you're with leans back in their chair, do the same. If one hand is in their pocket, follow suit. You are establishing a rapport with them. In other words, your energies are getting into synch. Once you do that, you can take control. Never do it obviously, or it will come off as mocking someone.

Energy works on a subconscious basis. So, subtlety is essential. It may take only a couple of seconds or an hour for you to lock energy, but once you do, you can test it by shifting yourself and seeing if they follow, or looking somewhere else to see if they look. Watch what happens when you change your position. Change your position and come closer to the table, and lower your voice slightly. Do they do the same? Remember, you don't have to do this *exactly* the way they do. For instance, if they put their hands up to their hair, you can just put it up to your forehead or face, the effect is still there.

A great example of effective mirroring is George Stroumboulopoulos' interview with Britney Spears. Knowing that she had been interviewed over 100 times that day alone, he knew that her defences were up, and she was prepared for the same redundant questions she had been receiving all day. He sat in his chair—sort of, middle of the chair, not too far back and not too far forward and whispered his questions to her. She leaned in and communicated back to him in the same way. Within 20 seconds of the interview, she had forgotten that there were cameras. She was emotionally involved in a private conversation just between the two of them.

Mirroring is a great technique to use on dates. Sitting in the restaurant, lock eyes with them. If they are explaining something and make a particular facial expression, follow it. If their hands are crossed in front of them, do the same.

Again, don't mirror obviously! It will come off as a mockery, or arrogance. Practice it with friends and family first. If they comment on it, you have done it obviously, if they don't, then enjoy the mutual energy you conjured. Incorporate breathing. You want to be able to breathe in synch with them. We want to keep rapport and lead the direction. So if you slow the breathing, if your pupils dilate, so will theirs. If you lower your voice and slow the speech pattern, so will they. When you lean in they will reciprocate. Once you slow it down, you bring an intimate feeling between the two of you.

Now, this technique can also work in a professional environment. For instance, there was an agent in LA that I wanted to work with. My first face to face meeting with the agent was in his office. The moment I entered, I saw a poster for "Gladiator" whereby he represented Ridley Scott, the director. I said right away (creating rapport) 'Wow, I loved Gladiator and have to say Ridley took an action movie premise and gave it so much depth! Congrats, that is a great client to have.' He smiled and looked at the poster for a moment which meant he was reflecting quickly on his relationship with Ridley. When we sat down, he looked at his computer to see any emails that came in the last 2 seconds, so I looked at my phone, which was off anyway, only to create a rapport. Then he sat back in his chair, so I leaned back in mine. Having already looked around his office, I saw pictures of him with many movie stars, and noticed he was always fashionably dressed and in great shape. So maintaining eye contact, I commented on how regimented his life was to be so dedicated to his work, and being physically fit. I added 'I am going to get into better shape'. He leaned forward (taking interest) and told me that he does yoga every morning and maybe

I should consider it. I nodded keeping a similar look on my face as he had on his, I answered that I should really look into it (hate yoga).

Now that I have locked energy, I am in synch, and we both are leaning in, I can now take control and take the lead. So I looked at the script in my hands, and his eyes went to the script. When I looked up at him, he did the same to me. When I reached out to give him the script, at the exact same second, he reached out to receive it. Even with the script in his hands, he didn't look at it, his contact was with my eyes. At the end of the meeting, he had heard every word I said, and he wanted to explore how we could work together like we were old friends.

■ EXERCISE

Subtly mirror someone, family, friend, date or mate. Start with first noticing the small movements and qualities about their body language. Then slowly and subtly start to go into the position they are in. Keep them talking or you talking to keep the attention away from what you are doing. When you do this, make sure you also look interested in what is being said and keep eye contact to make it harder for them to be distracted.

When they switch positions, do the same slowly and within 3 seconds of them doing it. Remember, it doesn't have to be exact, but similar positions. The brain will understand the similarities. Try and copy their breathing pattern. Hopefully they didn't just come in from a run, or you will look like a lunatic.

After about 2 minutes, start to change your position, and see if they follow. If they don't, that's ok, go back to the first part and try again. It just means you didn't take enough time to lock energy.

This exercise works like a yawn would when the one person witnesses it and then starts to do it themselves.

■ ■ ■ ■ ■ ■ ■ ■ ■ ■ ■ ■ ■ ■

CHAPTER TWO

The Preacher is NOT the Teacher

Remember that the most religious person at the table will never speak of religion. They understand what God is to them, and don't need to sell it to you. The two born-again Christian women that I know preach about what everyone is doing wrong but they themselves have one-night stands and drug addictions. However, they will go on, and on, and on about God.

To identify someone's biggest insecurities, listen to what they preach. Whether religious, happiness, wealth or philosophy. I will go as far as saying 98% of the time, they live the opposite. You may not see it at first, but if you keep watching it will reveal itself. I have a friend that used to brag about how fantastic his life and family were. When you asked how he was, he always said: 'Life is great, life is great!' He was so excited every time that it would get a little annoying. So, not wanting to but finally getting a little annoyed, I started to scrutinize his life. It turned out, he was away from his family four days out of seven and unwilling to change that. Eventually, the seam ripped, and his life was turned upside down when he discovered his wife was having an affair.

Today, when he says he is happy, I believe him, because he has come back down to earth and is more conscious of his emotions and the 'rose coloured glasses' he chose to wear.

Tip: The richest one at the table is the one who doesn't reach for the cheque the minute it comes. The poorest one is the one who reacts immediately.

So, if you find yourself talking a lot about how happy you are, or how well your career is going, or even how secure you are about yourself, ask yourself who you are trying to convince.

I love 'life coaches' and if you subscribe to my blog, you have seen how I have ripped the term to shreds. Some of the life coaches I have met are failed actresses that go to the next convenient thing! One life coach I heard from a friend that dated her, only eats 2 cupcakes a day to remain skinny! A life coach will almost always live the opposite of what they preach. Look for those that admit to their faults and show sincerity towards correcting them. There is also something about integrity. Do you want to be 'coached' by someone who has no integrity and tells you to do something they are not capable of?

I also love those who tell me how honest they are. I have met many businessmen who claim to be so honest, and have to remind me (more themselves) of that fact. Remember, the rules don't sometimes work on this one, they *always* work. Remember 'I am not a crook!' by Richard Nixon? That worked out well. What about the politicians that are not only against gay rights, but have to go on the biggest PR campaign to prove it? Or what about when I say I want to lose weight (clearly preaching, clearly).

This is a great technique when you want to know how to make the person feel secure and trust in you. For instance, if you get an actor that constantly has to tell you how great the director and casting agent thought he was, or the lawyer that has to go on and on about how they win every case, then you can just recite the key processing words back to them. 'Wow, you really committed to that character. You are a good actor!' Women do this to men they are interested or in love with. They become the emotional nurturer this way and we become reliant on their praises.

A female bodybuilder I know has in every line of her bio the fact she is 45 years old. Now it's great that she is able to keep her physique, but you can see that she is trying to sell herself on the fact that she is 'not' getting older by looking better and better against younger people. She is desperately trying to be praised for her youthful body. Turns out, she is one of many children, and probably didn't get as much attention as some of the others, so she is emotionally needy now. When she tried to retire from competition, she realized she had devoted all her attention and time to her body, and as a result no one knew her outside of bodybuilding.

CHAPTER 3

The Addiction Factor

All of us have an addiction that sits inside of us. The most fascinating are those addicted to "love". They are serial daters who are always in a relationship and always fall "head over heels" for the person they're with. They're actually head over heels for the endorphins they receive by being in that emotional state. Key to reading people is to pay attention to the addictions around, and potentially, in you.

I had a patient who came to me because her father died, her mother got cancer, and she calls herself "screwed up". After changing her perception of her mother's passing, giving her more appreciation for her father, and an understanding of how much further along she is than the real "screwed up people", she came back 6 months later telling me how screwed up she is because of the death of her parents. Nothing had changed. She was not loyal to any boyfriend, and she dulled her emotions through drug use. She was addicted to victimizing herself based on past experiences that had nothing to do with her fears and lack of motivation. An addiction like that is impossible to overcome until the person is ready to change.

Addiction is also found in the way of self sabotage. These are the people who constantly come up with excuses. I was coaching someone over Skype. She was based in Colombia and ran the South American operation of her family's company. She was not happy in her home, surroundings, business, or the fact she had to work with her ex-boyfriend. After spending 2 hours with her, she felt better.

The next day we spoke, and she had reverted right back to where she had been. Apparently she needed a ride, and the only person who could take her was the ex-boyfriend. She needed to use a phone and since hers was out of minutes, used his, only to see that he had called his new girlfriend 5 times. When I said that she needed to leave Colombia and go and see her family in Miami for a while, she came up with money excuses, travel timing excuses and then 'I don't know what I want' excuses. I knew then that it would not work. She was not ready to better herself and she had an addiction to feeling bad and like a 'loser', in her words.

Why? Not the point. We don't need to know why. We need to see it so we don't waste our time trying to push them in a direction or have expectations that won't come through. Remember, your job is to recognize the personality types and then use that to communicate TO them, not at them.

CHAPTER FOUR

Balance

When you fall madly in love, you are going to fall angrily out of love. The ideas that the Buddhists and the Hindus have been preaching for thousands of years, is to achieve a sense of balance. Anything to an extreme is a bad thing. Always remember to strive to maintain a balance.

I had just found out that Dr. John Demartini's book that we published was about to go into Amazon and bookstores. It was selling like hot cakes, and before the stores got the shipment, Barnes and Noble had ordered another 10,000 copies. It just so happens that I had to see him for lunch on the day I got the news, so I was going to give him the news in person. After telling him how excited I was we were going to be a number one book, his reply was, "Easy Sanjay. Calm down. You are on cloud nine and you will get knocked off. So, bring your fantasies down a notch". But, I thought what the hell does he know? This was my moment to shine, and I was going to savour every single moment of it.

I got in the car and started to drive home from our lunch. My cell phone rang as I got onto the highway. It was my distributor. My designer sent the wrong draft to the printer so all 15,000 copies were wrong with spelling errors, margin errors, and page errors. The profits from the book that we had made was spent pulling the books off the shelves and reprinting every copy. Now, this doesn't mean that the minute you experience success it will come crashing down, but it does mean that any time you lose your sense of reality, it will make itself known.

If I could go back in time, I would have enjoyed the fact we were getting a lot of attention from re-tailers, there was still a long road ahead, and that we had to plan the next step rather than sit and enjoy our little place on the hill.

Take a second today. If you're feeling low, balance it with a positive thought. No matter how low you are, or how depressed you are, find the positive, because it's there if you choose to see it.

CHAPTER FIVE

Success? No way!

Edmund Burgler, famous for his psychological theories, coined the saying: "pleasure in displeasure". Why are we poor? Why are we in bad relationships? And, why are we stuck in a hole that we can't seem to get ourselves out of? Is it luck? Is it smarts? Or, is it looks? The answer is none of the above.

I recently published a book titled "Making it in High Heels" which is a compilation of inspiring stories written by forty women. While on the cusp of getting a label deal, one of the participants wrote a great chapter about breaking into the music industry. The profits were going to charity and no one was getting paid. Nonetheless, she bickered and complained about the agreement, and after a long, drawn-out three days of negotiation, we decided to pull her story. I knew she was just afraid of success, and to this day she has not signed her label deal.

So, why do people choose not to achieve their potential? Most of us can't truly fathom success. It's not meant for us. It's meant for the lucky people. Our ego tries to protect us from failure by creating hurdles in front of our success.

Your preconceptions dictate your direction. BurmanBooks was only two years old when I decided I would go after the authors of "The Secret". Although they were the biggest motivational speakers in the world and I knew that other publishers 20 times the size of me had tried and failed, I decided I was going to sign them. There was no logic in signing with a small publisher who has yet to make a profit versus signing with a major billion dollar publisher. Still, without preconceptions, I courted them. The result was signing five out of the 10 speakers. If you let them, your preconceptions will disguise your ego and create failure.

It is amazing how many times in a day I speak to people that claim they want success and not only put nothing into action, they DO the exact opposite! For instance, I had a Miami based model come into town to see me about working together. She was a fitness model, TV host, actress and motivational speaker. My evaluation was that she was taking on anything out of desperation in hopes one would take off.

She went on to tell me how some producers try and sleep with her and others don't take her seriously because she has a great body and great looks. What I should explain is that she was wearing tight jeans, tiny top and lots of makeup. How did she expect people to react?

I was asked by someone who wanted a job if I knew anyone who was hiring. I made a few calls and got the person an interview at a private college as an office manager. Her reply was 'Thanks, but do you think they would allow me to work from home?' This is a conflict to anybody who truly wants success, and should be open to all opportunities in any form that it arrives in. This doesn't mean every opportunity has to be seized, but it does mean every opportunity should be investigated.

CHAPTER SIX

The word "No" is magical

Most people fear the word "no". In this chapter, you will learn how to turn the fear of no into the joy of yes. No is a temporary response to a long-term solution. No means nothing.

Dr. Joe Vitale is a hot author that I badly wanted to sign. Known for not only The Secret, but also a number of successful marketing books, I approached him numerous times. Each time was a definitive no. Every single time he said no, he or his assistant would give me a new explanation for their refusal. Rather than let their refusals dissuade me, I built a proposal that offered a solution to each of their perceived problems. It took four pitches, but I finally heard that lovely word. Yes, "Expect Miracles" by Dr. Joe Vitale was published by BurmanBooks.

If you associate "no" with rejection, incompetence or failure, you will build fantasies in your mind of what it means versus what the person is truly saying. My friend Ray Proctor loves the analogy when a waitress asks you if you would like dessert, and you say no, do they run and cry in the kitchen? The reason is it wasn't personal.

I have been told more no's than yes's. Yet I have been able to accomplish all my goals. Because when I hear no, I also hear persistence, results, and creative thinking. A no to me means I have not fully thought out, planned or executed a creative project. Not to get fancy, but it means I've been lazy. No is a reminder that I am not thinking outside of the box or envisioning an ideal solution. For me, no is just one step away from yes.

Try negotiating with someone even after they say no. Ask them why. Listen to their reasoning and formulate a new plan to motivate them to say yes. Remembering the rules you have learned so far, evaluate how they process information, what their motivation is, what are some of their interests to create rapport, lock in energy, and propose again. If at first you're not succeeding, try it again and again but don't talk at the person, talk to the person.

Listen to the reasoning for their refusal. Their reasoning is the key to changing their no into yes.

Always be thinking. If you run into a dead end, it doesn't mean it's the end of the road. I recently faced a financial wall. Books had to be delivered and the printing cost was high. We were financing a major PR tour for one of our authors and I still had to pay the bills. This was a very difficult time and I needed to think on my feet to avoid a disaster. I negotiated new terms with my printer since their intention was to keep me in business and continue getting my money and I was able to slow the authors tour down so he had time to rest and not feel so rushed and finally the bills I knew I could delay at least 20 days. Because of the events set in motion, the tour and books hit at a time the stock market crashed, causing more people to need motivation and feel secure about their lives! My apparent dead end quickly became a positive opportunity to help more people ending with positive results that not only gave me self-confidence, but also gave our company a much higher profile.

CHAPTER SEVEN

Our Unknown Heaven

Our fear comes from the unknown.

A general visits a prisoner the day before his execution. The general tells the prisoner he can choose between facing the firing squad or walking through a lone, unmarked door. The prisoner asks, "What's behind the door?" The general responds, "No one knows." The prisoner chooses execution. Afterwards, a soldier asks the general what was behind the door. The general responds, "Freedom."

We are so afraid of our unknown heaven, we choose to live in our known hell.

Fear is derived by our ego, which is located in the conscious front part of the brain. It's a security system that protects us and gives us self-worth, but also stops us from achieving our potential.

One of my clients is a criminal defence lawyer whose dream is to live in Trump Plaza. The fears of her past is the cement in front of her future.

117

My constant question to her is: the thought that is scaring you, does it get you closer to Trump Plaza? To combat your fears, focus on your goal. Have your goal written down and always visible. The reason they put blinders on horses when running races is because if a horse sees the number of other horses running beside it, it will get spooked and run circles. Create your own blinders so you only see your finish line.

Intimidation is just a lack of ownership of a part of yourself. When you are intimidated by a person, place, or thing, you are allowing that external element to take ownership over you. This will occur with a person you think is superior, in a job that you think is too successful, or while inhabiting an unfamiliar place. Lose the insecurity by asking yourself very specifically what it is you feel you are lacking that would make you otherwise equal.

Even though I really wanted to, I was always intimidated of producing a movie $20 million or higher in budget. Because of that, the industry had ownership over me. Once I asked myself why I was not attaining that budget level, I realized that I felt my experience did not equal the size of budget. Only at that point was I able to find clarity and collapse my insecurity, thereby regaining ownership over myself.

Do not use fictional or materialistic factors to overcompensate for your insecurity, since only two things will occur. One, you will look foolish and obvious, and two, it will not cure the problem.

For a time, because of my youth, I would have to negotiate against people 30 years my senior. They would often start the conversation by asking how old I was, and when I responded, they would laugh by responding I was as old as their children. This was a great way to demean me, knowingly or unknowingly, and intimidate me through their age and experience. Feeling that insecurity in myself, and lack of ownership over it, I gave them ownership over me by not only ignoring the problem and sometimes hiding from it, but masking it by shaving my head and growing a goatee to make me look older and more intimidating.

Nonetheless, I was still intimidated and even worse, it was obvious I was overcompensating for something. To collapse my insecurity, I had to realize I had a significant amount of experience and I was taught by good people. Most importantly though, I fixated on my goal. I kept my blinders on and focused on the end result. Slowly, the goatee and shaved head became less significant to me, and now I can say it is very difficult to intimidate me for any reason.

In confronting our fears, emotionally and spiritually, we win 100 percent of the time.

A friend of mine who has been married for six years and has two children constantly cheats on his wife. I asked him why he doesn't just confront her and tell her that he's no longer interested in being in a marriage. He said, "It's too complicated to split up and it's better for the kids if we're together". This was an obvious lie to himself. He was really afraid of being alone. It is obvious that children are better off in a two-parent household, but not with one parent being dishonest and deceitful to the other.

Do not allow your fear of the unknown get in your way. This, by far, would be the greatest tragedy you could ever experience.

Recipe for an ice cream cake that a family friend, Heather Scott, taught me patiently:

Buy a tub of chocolate ice cream, melt the whole thing, mix in two tubs of whipped cream and stir. Add in one tsp of coffee and 5 broken Crunchie bars, and mix all together. Pour into another dish and and sprinkle 1 crushed Scor bar over top. Freeze for 24 hours.

JOURNAL EXCERCISE

Talk to 10 people. When you have a general conversation, mark down the gestures you see them make in regards to the conversation. Also make note of the type of words they use and evaluate them as being aesthetic, audible or kinesthetic. Once you get in the habit of doing this, it will become easier and easier.

Person #1

■ GESTURES   **■ VERBIAGE**

_____   _____

_____   _____

_____   _____

_____   _____

_____   _____

_____   _____

_____   _____

_____   _____

_____   _____

_____   _____

_____   _____

_____   _____

Person #2

■ GESTURES　　　　　**■ VERBIAGE**

_____	_____
_____	_____
_____	_____
_____	_____
_____	_____
_____	_____
_____	_____
_____	_____
_____	_____
_____	_____
_____	_____
_____	_____

Person #3

GESTURES

VERBIAGE

_____   _____

_____   _____

_____   _____

_____   _____

_____   _____

_____   _____

_____   _____

_____   _____

_____   _____

_____   _____

_____   _____

_____   _____

_____   _____

Person #4

■ GESTURES

■ VERBIAGE

_____

_____

_____

_____

_____

_____

_____

_____

_____

_____

_____

_____

_____

Person #5

■ GESTURES   **■ VERBIAGE**

_____   _____

_____   _____

_____   _____

_____   _____

_____   _____

_____   _____

_____   _____

_____   _____

_____   _____

_____   _____

_____   _____

_____   _____

Person #6

■ GESTURES   **■ VERBIAGE**

_____   _____

_____   _____

_____   _____

_____   _____

_____   _____

_____   _____

_____   _____

_____   _____

_____   _____

_____   _____

_____   _____

_____   _____

_____   _____

Person #7

■ GESTURES   ■ VERBIAGE

_____   _____

_____   _____

_____   _____

_____   _____

_____   _____

_____   _____

_____   _____

_____   _____

_____   _____

_____   _____

_____   _____

_____   _____

Person #8

■ GESTURES   **■ VERBIAGE**

_____   _____

_____   _____

_____   _____

_____   _____

_____   _____

_____   _____

_____   _____

_____   _____

_____   _____

_____   _____

_____   _____

_____   _____

_____   _____

Person #9

■ GESTURES   **■ VERBIAGE**

_____   _____

_____   _____

_____   _____

_____   _____

_____   _____

_____   _____

_____   _____

_____   _____

_____   _____

_____   _____

_____   _____

_____   _____

Person #10

■ GESTURES

■ VERBIAGE

_____   _____

_____   _____

_____   _____

_____   _____

_____   _____

_____   _____

_____   _____

_____   _____

_____   _____

_____   _____

_____   _____

_____   _____